Tough Turf

MADE EASY

for

The INDIAN

Stock Market

INVESTORS

&

TRADERS

© CA Lakshminarayanan R

March 04, 2016

1.   Purpose

Indian Stock Market was intended to provide liquidity to the investors. However the fundamentals have changed over the years. Stock Market has now become a place for those seeking quick money.

This write-up does not deal with the technical analysis or the analytical parameters such as, Relative Share Index, Moving Averages, Bollinger Bands, Directional Index, Parabolic Stop Reversal, etc.

Also, this write-up is not intended to provide advice on buy or sell of equity, equity derivatives or mutual funds.

Going by the wild market movements with higher price spreads before and after the parliamentary and state elections, budgets, confidence motions, passing of bills etc., I sometimes wonder if the Indian Stock Market is by and for the politicians and whether it is a PTM (Politicians' Teller Machine), for use whenever felt necessary.

This in a way may be a, Make in India, to help Indian individuals investing and trading in the Indian Stock Market equities, equity derivatives and Mutual Funds. In the coming days I wish to do more research in this area and come out with my observations.

Next Market and the participants

2.   Market and the participants

Indian Stock Market has an average turnover of around Rupees 100,000 crores a day, from trading in the equity and derivative segments, across the National and Bombay Stock Exchanges.

It helps the Government get several crores service tax in a year.

FII/ FPI & DII

Trading activity on the NSE, BSE and MSEI
On Capital Market segment

Foreign Institutional Investors (FII)/ Foreign Portfolio Investors (FPI), trading activity on NSE, BSE and MSEI on Capital Market segment

The following is combined FII/FPI trading data across NSE, BSE and MSEI collated on the basis of trades executed by FIIs/FPIs

FII/FPI trading activity on NSE, BSE and MSEI in capital market segment (Rs Crores) for 04-March-2016

Category	Buy Value	Sell Value	Net Value
FII/FPI	4,231.60	3,560.03	671.57

Domestic Institutional Investors trading activity on NSE, BSE and MSEI on Capital Market segment

The following is combined Domestic Institutional Investors data across NSE, BSE and MSEI collated on the basis of trades executed by Banks, Insurance, MFs and New Pension System

DII trading activity on NSE, BSE and MSEI in capital market segment (Rs Crores) for 04-March-2016

Category	Buy Value	Sell Value	Net Value
DII	1,393.43	1,926.53	-533.10

**Instrument wise volume and turnover
March 04, 2016, 15:30:45 IST**

Product	Number of Contracts	Turnover INR (Rs crores)	Premium Turnover (Rs crores)
Index futures	3,18,830	16,212.56	
Index options	5,98,287	26,541.63	
Stock futures	29,36,926	1,59,713.85	1,591.60
Stock options	3,07,486	13,728.27	380.41
F & O Total	**41,61,529**	**2,16,196.32**	**1,972.01**

Majority, that is, more than 90% of the turnover is from the equity derivative segment.

There are around 8,600 registered FPI and Deemed FPIs as per the NSDL website. There are more than 8,000 mutual fund schemes.

NSDL
Technology Trust and Reach

Per NSDL website (around March 04, 2016)

https://www.fpi.nsdl.co.in/web/Reports/ReportsListing.aspx
https://www.fpi.nsdl.co.in/web/Reports/RegisteredFIISAFPI.aspx

FPI Monitor

Home >> FPI/FII Investments >> View Report

List of Registered FPIs/ Deemed FPIs

I.   FPIs   4,003 records

II.   Deemed FPIs
      (Erstwhile FIIs)   1,007 records

III. Deemed FPIs
      (Erstwhile Sub-Accounts)   3,678 records

There are around 1,44,83,000 investor accounts per NSDL website as at February 29,2016

https://nsdl.co.in/

NSDL
National   Securities Depository Limited

Statistics

Investor Accounts   -   1,44,83,434

DP Service Centres   -   26,187

Demat Custody Value -   109,06,227
INR (Rs) in crores

US Dollars equivalent
      US $ in billion   -   1,589

BSE (Bombay Stock Exchange) website
http://www.bseindia.com/
states that, there are more than
3,05,68,000 as registered investors
around Feb 29, 2016

Market Statistics

Market Capitalization of BSE Listed Cos. (Rs Crores)		86,34,614
Registered Investors (Nos.)		3,05,68,408
No. of Companies Traded		2,653
Advances	1,005	
Declines	1,481	
Unchanged	167	
Total No. of orders		22,82,57,002
Equity orders	21,12,59,284	
Derivative orders	1,06,21,368	
Currency and Interest Rate orders	63,76,350	

BSE (Bombay Stock Exchange) website
http://www.bseindia.com/

Listing Statistics (around Feb 29, 2016)

a. No. of Cos. with listed equity capital   5,446

    Suspended   1,520

    Available for trade   3,926

    Permitted to trade   70

    Total available for trade   3,996

b. No. of companies
    with only debt capital listed   318

c. No. of AMCs –
    Mutual Fund Schemes Listed   23

Total no. of listed entities (a + b + c)   5,787

Foreign Portfolio or Foreign Institutional Investors (FII) and Domestic Institutional Investors (DII), together account for more than 90% of the market turnover. Less than 10% of the turnover could be attributed to the trading and investing by the individuals.

But taking 10% of the total turnover in the futures and options segment alone as per NSE website provide 21,619 crores. On an average, if an individual trades for Rs 15,000 in the F&O segment, then 1.45 crores investor accounts will be providing a turnover of Rs 21,750 crores a day.

At 3% loss of that turnover, every day on an average, each individual may be losing around Rs 450 a day. That is 450 x 225 days = Rs 1,01,250 loss per individual per year.

Even taking Rs 1,00,000 loss per individual it is 145,000 crores loss to the individual segment which is nothing but profits to the FII. FPI and DIIs

If the Indian Stock Market is by and for the politicians not caring for public welfare and for those rich evading taxes, then their excesses may have a nexus with the stock market operations directly or indirectly.   Next > Market Mechanism

3.   Market Mechanism

Though gaining or winning is a subjective term, anyone who comes to the market, invest and trade, do so, only to gain and maximize wealth.

There are winners and losers. Per the market mechanism, every rupee lost by one is gained by the other and this is there on every trade at any point of time.

However, there is a great imbalance in the system that provides mostly losses to one class of investors, estimated to be numbering more than 1,25,00,000 (one crore twenty five lakhs) from the individual retail segment.

Retail individuals invest and trade either with their borrowed funds or hard earned savings.

As per the Bombay Stock Exchange (BSE) website there are more than 3 crore registered investors. As per the NSDL website there are around 1.45 crore investor accounts.

No investor protection fund, or authorities, howsoever paid they are by the public funds, could either prevent or devise a concrete system to minimize the loss of retail investors.

Up next   Retail investors

4.   Retail Investors

Going by the statistics of registered investors in the BSE and NSDL, out of around 1.45 crores registered investors, there should be more than 1.25 crore individual investors investing and trading in the Indian stock market.

Majority of the individual investors, trading either in the equity segment or in the equity derivative segment are on the losing side.

At least 1 crore retail investors are attached to in the stock market system, are presumed to be not related to those who fix the prices of scrips at any given point of time, according to their whims and fancies with their money might and power clout.

Average loss for an individual retail investor through equity and equity derivatives may be around Rs 100,000 (rupees one lakh or hundred thousand) in a year, meaning a loss of 1 lakh crores in a year for the retail investors which would be profits mostly for the FIIs.

My endeavor through this is to provide a system that could safeguard, protect and reduce the loss by at least 1/10th of that figure that is 10% of Rs 1,00,000 being Rs 10,000 per annum per individual retail investor of our country, thereby saving them and for the country Rs 10,000 crores or rupees hundred billion saving in a year.

(Rs. 10,000 x 10,000,000 investors
= Rs 100,000,000,000)

Next Investors are traders?

5.   Any investor is also a trader

Investment need not necessarily be in direct monetary terms. Time has a money value.

So, there is an investor always in anyone, particularly with all those in the stock market.

The objective for monetary investments for any, is only to make a gain from them.

None may want to park his/her money in the stock market for ego.

But in general that is what happens; people like what they did and love what they have and holding onto what they have, aspire and go for what they want.

Investments are not to be driven by ego.

Some people take pride holding on to some assets, like balance with a particular bank, holding a blue chip stock, investor in a particular mutual fund, having a property in a particular location, holding a particular brand vehicle, and so on.

In general, people buy and hold shares in listed companies only to sell for a profit at a later point of time.

Next Where do individuals invest?

6.   Where do individuals invest?

Individual investments vary from person to person according to their taste, preference, and risk appetite.

Some are happy to keep them in Savings bank account for safety and liquidity while others keep some part of that in recurring or term deposits.

Some use their savings to invest in the money back or endowment policies, while others go to Government Securities or real estate, for tax savings.

Those that are lured by the positive returns from the stock market, get into it, directly or through the Mutual Funds, to invest in the best of the schemes that are offered.

For some of the stock market investors, once they get into a particular investment, then particularly when in loss, either their ego rides them to say what they did was right, if their moves were by themselves, or their broker tells them to wait if their actions were due to the brokerage recommendations.

Brokers get their income, whether one buys or sells at a loss or profit.

Next How do individuals invest?

7. How do individuals invest?

Individuals are driven to the Stock Market by a variety of forces and factors.

Those who are following the news papers, TV channels, commentaries of experts, recommendations of brokers, suggestions by friends and relatives, get attracted by the lucrative returns from the stocks and mutual funds.

They get into either cash or derivative segment or into mutual funds, depending upon their risk appetite, expecting to get a better return than their bank deposits.

In the derivative segment, they take a position, either buy or sell in futures or options by impulse or per advice from experts and consultants.

Majority of the individual investors see themselves on the losing side, with sudden and wild market movements that impact their holdings and resources with unreasonable and higher magnitudes, like earthquake or Tsunami.

Next Living with the moves

8. Living with the moves, tolerance

For some of the stock market investors, once they get into an investment, then either their ego takes over them or their broker tells them to wait and hold.

When prices move in the opposite direction, those that are emotional either live with decaying hope or exit at loss sensing hopeless situations.

Brokers get their income, whether one buys or sells at a loss or profit.

Mutual Funds get their administration charges and Banks are helped by the cash float that flows in the process, on which they do not have to pay any interest to the investor.

Most of the individual investors would be hearing from time to time that there is no relation between performance of the entity and its share price in the market as many extraneous factors influence the market price.

But what those extraneous factors that could influence the market price even fundamentally strong stocks, resulting in a loss to retail investors?

What the individuals want is profit, but most of them, affected by the frequent market volatility or turbulence, knowingly or unknowingly, make and live with, real and notional losses, with opportunity cost of time and money and other associated costs. An example of tolerance, a term that is much talked about these days in the media.

Up next   Do fundamentals work?

9.   Do fundamentals work?

Every investor is also a trader and many follow the fundamentals of scrip. They buy scrip for selling it later at a higher price and sell scrip at a higher price to buy the same at a lower price.

Human psychology is first to buy and then sell. Big players play with this retail investor psychology and push the prices down by shorting.

Most of the individual investors in the cash segment, also trade in equity derivatives. They buy futures, call or put options to sell them for a profit or loss.

If one observes in the stock market movements, for most of the stocks, upward price movements occur, lesser number of times or with lower magnitude as compared to their movement downwards.

And those following fundamentals, may feel hurt at those times, whenever there is a market crash for several attributed and unrealistic reasons.

No matter what the fundamentals are, prices get manipulated as could be deciphered from a trader's experience with scrip named IFCI Ltd., BSE Code 500106 and NSE Code INE039A01010 recently on 3rd February 2016, mentioned under the heading number 20.

Next: Are brokers too concerned about your profits?

10. **Are brokers so concerned about your profits and wealth?**

Why should experts give free profitable advice to traders?

Why should brokers provide stock buy or sell recommendations to their clients? Agreed, they will get brokerage and commission on sale of IPOs, Mutual fund and insurance products.

What else?

Would they be concerned that their clients should get financially richer by making more profits?

They may not be, because if their clients are making profits who would be those losing? FIIs? DIIs? Retail investors with other brokers?

They may have to meet their quota to arrange clients who would follow their buy or sell recommendations as someone else, big trader, may want to sell or buy a particular quantity at a particular price.

Obviously when people buy and sell there is a market action, and other innocent individual investors participate and an artificial market volume and movement comes up.

Individual retail investors fall prey to it and get stuck up.

Whatever be the name of the equity scheme or the mutual fund, growth fund, maximiser fund, advantage fund, in general they may not be for the retail investors and may have been intended only for the growth, advantage of those wanting to maximise their wealth at the cost of the retail investors.

If the brokers are for the retail investors not to lose, then who are losing? FIIs? DIIs?

Apparently it is the retail investors who would be mostly on the losing side, on subjective terms.

Next Market Movement

11. Market Movement

Whatever be the external or extraneous attributed unrealistic reasons for the fall and rise of share prices, unless the big players are involved, price movement and market action would be minimum.

Price and volume creating cartels are the market movers.

They decide which way they would move the indices, constituent stocks, and the prices of stocks not associated with the indices either in tandem with the indices or opposite to the movement of the indices.

Overbought and oversold levels are easily taken care of by small downward movements and upward movements respectively.

News flow, opinion polls, positive or negative and interpretation by the analysts and experts only fool the average retail investors and traders.

They could easily be controlled by the persons having vested interests according to the way they want the same to be, same as the way they could pre-determine the price movements.

Your trades are not secret. Executives in the brokerage firms could share, particularly your F&O trades with cartels.

Artificial volumes may get created in the F&O and the operators could know what position their side hold and they easily get to know what are the positions held by those not in their network.

They could work to get, those not in their radar, out at a loss, and know easily to which brokerage, investor traders not in their network, belong to, through the brokerage desks.

The questions that one gets is, are the market movements artificial, and directed by some? If so, who are they and for whom do they do so?

Next Why only individuals (retail investors) mostly make losses?

12. Why individuals make mostly losses?

Each counter, particularly around 160 going by the number of stocks in the F&O segment may have a head broker and that broker may get trading data from the other brokers and sub-brokers, share and know those that are not in their network, arrange to move the prices such that the persons not in their network get out with a loss, providing profit for the operators.

.

Covered term is, "Dealing Room"??

An investor cum trader was astonished that positions taken by him on his own in the futures and options segment, and held by s/he was well known to his broker representative and there is every possibility that the information may get shared with the concerned cartels.

Therefore, anyone's trade may not be secret and therefore not necessarily known only to that person.

If an individual is offered a buy of a scrip for a profit, who would sell that at a loss?

Either the one who is in desperation to sell or the one who has bought at a price much lower, or the one that has no idea. Desperation rarely occurs, and occurs at times of a big crash with traders.

Executives in the brokerages may share, particularly your F&O trades with cartels.

Next, External extraneous factors, are they internal?

13. External extraneous internal factors

Here is an example for the so called external extraneous internal factors influencing the market price, Wed., 3rd Feb 2016.

The share price of IFCI Ltd., a Government Company, listed in BSE and NSE fell from 23.05 to 21.50 in 15 minutes between 13:00 hours and 13:15 hours on Wednesday, 3rd February 2016.

With the book value of the company keep increasing with its profits quarter over quarter, company paying dividend year after year, generally no single or group of individual investor/s would have sold so many leading to such a sudden fall in the prices.

The price spread, amounting to Rs. 1.55 at 6.70% fall per share within 15 minutes seemed very artificial and supposed to be backed by some price cartel to benefit someone as there is no corresponding adverse announcement to the effect, or any downside movement in the index, even if one were to associate the movement with the index movement.

IFCI Ltd. Cash Price
(03/02/2016 02:04:59) at
The NSE (National Stock Exchange)
Scrip Code ISIN: **INE039A01010**

-0.75
-3.28%

Open	High	Low
22.40	23.50	21.50

LTP	Previous Close	VWAP
22.10	22.85	22.81

The information above shows IFCI Cash price on 03 Feb 2016 around 2.05pm. There is a vast difference of Rs 0.71 (3.11%) between the then last traded price LTP of Rs 22.10 and the volume weighted average (VWAP) price of Rs 22.81

Nifty moved from Rs 7397.40 to 7390.90 during the same time with a drop of only 6.50 points or around 0.09%.

Did IFCI Ltd. stock price get manipulated?

We have just read that on 3rd February 2016, the share price of IFCI Ltd., fell from 23.05 to 21.50 in 15 minutes between 13:00 hours and 13:15.

Further, within that 15 minutes period, in particular, in 5 minutes between 13:10 and 13:15 hours surprisingly the price fell from 22.60 to 21.50. That is a fall of 4.86% or Rs 1.10 within 5 minutes!

Again, it was on 10th Feb 2016. IFCI Ltd., moved from Rs. 23.55 to 22.20, with a fall of Rs 1.35 per share or 5.73% just in 30 minutes between 9.15 am and 9.45 am. Close price at 9.45 am was Rs 22.40 and the value weighted average was around 22.70 that is 1% more than the close!

Same day, between 15:15 and 15:20 hours the movement was between 22.10 and 21.50 , i.e. 2.71% or Rs 0.60 fall in 5 minutes. Presumably someone or more, with those price spreads got benefited, with the operators helping the movement.

If the share price of a Government Company, in the Futures and Options segment, could fall around 5% within 5 minutes, could it fall 100% within 120 minutes or 2 hours !?!

Next > Price fixing?

14.   Price Fixing?

The Central Government through the President has majority holding in IFCI Ltd., on behalf of the Indian public.

If a Government Company, IFCI's equity share prices could be subject to large scale manipulation, as was apparent from its share price movement on 3rd February 2016, i.e. falling from 23..05 to 21.50, in 15 minutes between 13:00 hours and 13:15 hours what could not be possible with other stocks in general, if external or extraneous forces act.

It only states that the price could be fixed by some forces at any time according to their whims and fancies.

Could not SEBI, NSE, BSE or the Finance Ministry easily unearth the reasons and the people behind?

With the power, position, infrastructure they have, they could, but they may not, either fully or partly, for their own best known reasons, because they are for safeguarding the public interest?

What extraneous external factors that could influence the market price, resulting in a sudden loss to the individual retail investor?

There will be responses from the company stating that they do not have any say about the market price or its determinants.

So the existence of extraneous external or internal forces deciding the market prices is apparent, but how to get the resources of Indian retail investors protected?

15.   The Enigmatic Riddle

Another example is the price movement of scrip the NTPC Ltd. Why should any valuable Government owned stock, either it is BHEL or NTPC, fall before, and whenever, there is a stake sale.

Could it be that persons make profit in futures and options segment, as desired and bring that as investment?

Could there not be better ways for the Government to get their assets monetized for more values?

Do not the concerned assets have greater value, when any new company that comes with initial public offering is priced very high?

Examples of recent public offerings, Quick Heal Technologies at Rs 321, Teamlease Services at Rs 850, Precision Camshafts at Rs 186.

How is the SEBI allowing such initial public offerings at such prices when long existing profit making, dividend paying, Government companies are getting traded at less than their book values?

An enigmatic riddle and none in the Governmental system seems to be doing anything to control this aspect.

Next, Who helps who?

16.   Who helps WHO?

Recently the government was selling 41,22,73,220 equity shares in NTPC via offer-for-sale (OFS) Floor price for the offer is fixed at Rs 122, a 3.8 percent discount to Monday's closing price of Rs 126.85.

NTPC's two-day offer for sale has opened for subscription on 23 February 2016.

There could be better terms for the Government to get greater value for its holdings or stake transfer. Greater value means better for the people and the country.

Instead of offer for sale, could it not be offer for partnership? Not that the company will get into partnership as per law. Shareholders are after all, partners in profits, positive or negative. Are not they?

NTPC stock price went down by more than 5% since the start of the stake sale or offer for sale by the Government.

Government's 5 percent stake sale was approved by the Cabinet in May 2015.

NTPC was quoting around Rs 145 between Dec 2015 and Jan 2016. Government was selling NTPC shares around 125.

Why did not the Government sell when NTPC was quoting around 145? Was it a desperate sale? If so, why and how things were taken to a desperate level?

Was not Rs 20 per share on 41.22 crore shares then offered for sale, valuing more than 800 crores important for the Government.

Will anyone, not at any desperation to sell, sell their personal assets, do so at such levels?

Who are the beneficiaries?

FIIs or DIIs?

Who are those FIIs and DIIs?

Next Expect reasons, they are expert reasons

17.   Expert Reasons

Indices in the Indian Stock Market move up and down with the movement in the constituent scrips.

An orchestra comprising FIIs, DIIs, television channels, websites, experts, and brokerages help the market movement as desired by some, attributing unreasonable reasons reasonably! driving the retail investors to further investment and trades, either on the long or on the short sides.

Longing for gains, individuals, in general, find their financial resource shorter, either notional or real, than what that was earlier.

Proclaimed stock market experts have four hands, two forehands and two back hands.

Because whenever they give their views on any aspect, they would start saying, *"on one hand I think…….. and on the other hand I think ……."* and they would *then use their other two hands, by extending "having said that", "on one hand I think ……. and on the other hand I think ……"* and the number of hands would keep growing as the hands would be different every next time.

If the market price of any scrip is going up, majority of their voices would be in favour of a further up move.

If a stock price has to go up, despite poor results, they would highlight something as the most positive, compare the results of year over year instead of quarter over quarter, and even though the operations and results are not seasonal.

Financial results may be depicted tremendously to state that they have either beaten or were below estimates without explaining the details and computations of such estimates.

90% of the market movement is by the FIIs and DIIs and only less than 10% participation is from the retail investors' side and within that there would be those connected with the vested interests.

DIIs are mostly made up of Mutual Funds and Insurance companies.

Mutual Funds have assets under management of more than 12 lakh crores.

Retail investors get misled by the so called bulk deals, buy backs, and offer for sale or opinion polls.

Now the question comes, who are the FIIs? Why should they invest so much in Indian Stock Market? Will they like India to grow more than their country?

Next Foreign Institutional Investors (FIIs)

18. Foreign Portfolio or Foreign Institutional Investors (FIIs)

When an individual suffers, in general, neither his (her) neighbors, relatives, friends, nor the Governmental systems, believe in, care, come to the rescue and help that person.

If such is the case, how could and why would, a person of a foreign country be interested and investing in India?

When they have a problem in their own country, why should they invest in India?

With exceptions, there may not be many foreign institutional investors in general.

It may be the name for the country's unaccounted money escaping tax that takes the colour of foreign institutional investor, worldwide wherever there is large scale corruption.

We hear and read about accumulation of wealth by politicians across the world.

At best what they could do with them? Spending for elections, publicity, funding the vote bank, accumulates asset in direct and indirect names, enjoy the best of the comforts in life at will, and so on.

Using them for and through stock market operations with the colour of foreign institutional investors maximise their resources and gets them a great social status.

Now let us see our
Domestic Institutional Investors (DIIs)

19.   Domestic Institutional Investors

Unaccounted money remaining abroad may have been used through the Stock Market, for multiplying them for a better funding in the elections and publicity.

Prices are moved up and down according to their whims and fancies with the orchestra of television channels, expert voices, websites, brokerages, etc.

Domestic Institutional Investors (DIIs) are Mutual Funds, Domestic Financial Institutions, Insurance companies, etc. managing over Rs. 12 lakh crores.

With exceptions, they may generally be helping the cause of Foreign Insitutional Investors participating in the turnover build-up and pricing mechanism.

Domestic institutional investors with the level of money under their management should be making big profits. Are they?

Individual retail investors lose their hard earned savings and borrowed monies.

Average of loss of a individual retail investor may be at least Rs 1,00,000 in a year meaning a loss of at least Rs 1,00,00,00,00,000 (one lakh crores) in the retail individual investor segment which may be a profit for the other, mostly for the Foreign Portfolio or Institutional Investors.

Let's go to see some funny new headlines

20. Funny headlines and possible meanings

I wonder, if the market moves are dictated and hidden in the pre-market headlines that one could see in some media.

Some of the notable and funny headlines observed are:

On policy day, look to North Block, not Mint Street

One could sense that the movement upward (north) would be blocked, directing a go short and signaling a downward movement.

That is one should not think of making or minting money in the expectation of prices moving up, meaning that the prices would go down.

Nifty can fall at opening, Nifty <u>can gain</u> at opening bell, Nifty <u>can open</u> in green

What is the meaning of the word **can?**

Are there directions to the operating cartels, whether bull or bear? Operators may be the same, they may be called bulls at times and bears at times, from time to time.

Is there no difference between the words "can" "may"?

Nifty likely to start in the green, Nifty likely to open gap down,

Nifty likely to open in red, Nifty to follow global cues

Are these suggesting that the price movements are being fixed.

Reasons for market moves are attributed. Either crude oil prices going up or down, US markets trading down or higher, DAX, CACs, Nikkei or Shanghai trading lower or higher, should not affect the Indian Market, unless the players are the same or inter-related or associated.

21. F&O
Futures and Options segment

Television channels, experts, analysts, say fresh longs, fresh shorts, unwinding, short covering, call writing, put writing etc.

For every buy position there is a sell position.

In other words, whatever one sells the other buys.

How can someone write a call or put without a buyer? What is long for one is short for the other.

So how could there be fresh shorts or fresh longs?

Fresh shorts or fresh longs only state that those in the known network are taking positions in the direction of the desired price movement.

That means cartels play, keep the underlying or the future and option prices, at a particular level with a desired volume, among themselves and induce the retailers to get into and get in between, for the cartels to exit at a profit, through the expert voices and brokerages.

One may see at times, that a price of scrip hardly moves significantly and moves within a very small range for a few hours, days or weeks.

That may be because, from that level either the price would be taken up or brought down to a wanted level, at a desired time for some preferred period by some interested.

When one could see that for one stock, such a scenario may be there with most of the stocks that are traded, from time to time.

Retail investors and traders mostly long for the loss of money.

So, how to safeguard the retail investors?

Why should the retail investors or traders be funding the profits of Foreign Institutional Investor status holding traders?

So, let's see if the individual retail investors and traders could be protected by some way beyond any investors' protection fund as that is only any bank's safe deposit.

22. Safeguarding Individual
retail investors and traders

Market manipulation cannot be stopped as there would always be greedy insiders who may gain through ways indecipherable by the tough or lenient authorities.

I have a solution for that also, which could save crores of money loss for the retail investors, but that need encouragement and financial support from the individual retail investor community and the Government.

There would always be some among the individual retail investors who may be closer to the management, insiders, FIIs and politicians and not falling within the definition of relatives.

Nevertheless, the losses could be minimized for the individual retail investors if,

There is a separate window for the trading of the in BSE and NSE for both equity and derivative products, as applicable, for the

a.   Honorable President, Central and State Governments (representing Indian citizens for their holdings), Domestic Trusts and Foundations

b.   individual retail investors

c.	Domestic Institutional Investors (comprising Mutual Funds, Indian Financial Institutions, Banks, Insurance Companies, NBFCs and Corporate houses) and Indian promoters

d.	Foreign Institutional Investors (comprising foreign pension funds, foreign portfolio investors, overseas bodies corporate, foreign promoters)

Trading volumes may be lower in the retail segment but the trading would be healthier. Loss of retail investors would reduce and loss for any individual investor(s) would only be profit for the other individual investor(s) and not for the FIIs or the DIIs.

DIIs will be more responsible in their trading and handling public funds.

DII and retail investors' money would remain within the country and foreign exchange rates would be less affected in this regard.

FIIs will trade within them and the profits and loss would be only between them and their trading will not affect the DIIs or the individual retail investors.

Stock fundamentals would get respect from investors.

There would be more meaningful level playing field for various investor categories based on their financial strength.

Bank finance for pledged shares to be provided only up to 50% of the respective company's book value through tangible assets, and not based on market values to help prevent mass selling by the promoters or the banks, to recover the bank dues, affecting the prices in the process, though banks and promoters would be in the same platform.

Though there could be price differences between the windows for individual retail investors, DIIs and FIIs, it would remain so and will not affect values in either of the windows.

For example, there is a difference between the market price of IDRs of Standard Chartered Bank traded in INR in India and the value of its equity shares traded in GBP in the UK.

They remain so and neither affects the trading of the other. 10 IDRs in INR equal one equity share in GBP (Great Britain Pound)

Who am I, thinking and writing like this?

23.   About Me

Am a Chennai based Indian CA with over 10 years experience of trading in equities and equity derivatives.

This write-up is from my experience and the passion for the nationals.

I have 1 equity share in more than 2,500 companies listed in the BSE and NSE, intended for a Financial SystemSURGERY.

If many would do so, it will help reduce unreasonable market price volatility.

I was holding 1 equity share in more than 3,350 companies in May 2014 and I had to sell some 850 company shares to meet financial difficulties.

By holding a share in the companies engaged in various business activities, I indirectly have some part of lands, buildings, tea coffee estates, building products, parks, theatres, hospitals, medical and surgical equipments, hotels, restaurants, SPA, cars, motorcycles, bicycles, jeeps, tractors, earth movers, vehicle service providers, petrol, diesel, machineries, roads, bridges, aircrafts, railway wagons, ships, buses, of various brands, furniture, refrigerators, heating, lighting and ventilation equipments, towel, dresses, beds, blankets, pillows, carpets, official and casual footwear, eye wear, tooth paste, tooth brush, soap, cleaning items, cosmetics, shaving products, salt, sugar, food items, coffee, tea, water, jewelries, gold, silver ornaments, crockery, cutlery, household items, desktops, laptops, books, stationery, mobiles, watches, medicines, precious and semi-precious metals, gas, oil, cash, etc. across India, being those remaining as assets (inventory) in the books of the respective companies that individuals need and use from, top to bottom, raise to rest, on any day.

Am happy that my holdings give work and revenue, as applicable for 2,500 company registrars, printers, publishers, bankers, courier operators, postal department, in terms of corporate communications, dividend pay-outs, etc.

Going forward, with the blessings of The GOD, I wish to embark in other areas of public importance to make them better with surgery, without knife.

I have already published a basic level work for democracy in and through LetsValue website.

Views expressed in the write-up are my personal and are not intended to hurt any particular person or group of persons or organization(s).

If an audit report or a medical report, or a legal opinion or a professional CV writing, have a value, the contents of this write-up, may be worth more than the value sought, for this book or write-up and I believe the reader feels that.

This book is a system surgery of the Indian stock market operations, from my perspective to be educative for any existing or prospective investor or trader in the Indian Stock Market.

I request the encouragement and support of the IIITs (Indian Individual Investors & Traders)

Pricing

It is a national service.

Trying to save a loss of Rs 145000,00,00,000 (Rs 1,45,000 crores) for the individual segment, even if I take 0.001% of that or 1/100000 it works out to Rs 1.45 crores.

However much I wish, though not all 1,45,00,000 investors and traders will buy this and only 0.5% of them or 1 in every 200 individuals may buy this.

So, am pricing this conservatively per copy expecting some 72,500 individuals across the country to buy this.

If anyone feels that the price of this write-up is on the higher side, they may please advise me the price that s/he was willing to pay and I will return the difference.

Requesting you to be one of the expected 14,500 individuals across the country, I welcome comments, and could be contacted through Mobile +919884034404 or e-mail LEMINAR@GMail.com